When Your

Adult Children
Don't Go to Mass

Sallie Latkovich, CSJ

Liguori

Imprimi Potest: Harry Grile, CSsR
Provincial, Denver Province, The Redemptorists

Published by Liguori Publications
Liguori, Missouri 63057, USA
To order, call 800-325-9521, Liguori.org

ISBN 978-0-7648-1990-2

Liguori Publications, a nonprofit corporation,
is an apostolate of the Redemptorists
(redemptorists.com).
Cover design: John Krus
Cover image: Dean Drobot, Shutterstock
Printed in the United States of America

22 21 20 19 18 / 7 6 5 4 3

When Your Adult Children Don't Go to Mass

Sallie Latkovich, CSJ

One of the most frequent questions faithful Catholic parents ask is, "My adult children don't go to Mass. What can I do?"

In this pamphlet, I'll address four aspects of this dilemma: 1) the guilt and betrayal parents and grandparents feel when their adult children and grandchildren no longer go to Mass; 2) why adult children stop going to Mass; 3) what you can and can't do to bring them back; and 4) how to keep from losing heart.

The prayer at the end of the pamphlet will help you ask God for the strength to live with your children's choices, never letting them forget how much you love them, even when you can't affirm their actions.

Guilt and Betrayal: The Feelings of Faithful Parents and Grandparents

Parents and grandparents often take responsibility for their adult children's choices. If they disagree with the choice, they assume they did something wrong as parents, and they feel guilty.

At the same time, parents and grandparents who value their faith and continue to be active members of their parish communities often feel betrayed when their children no longer go to church.

Guilt and betrayal are painful. They rise up as their children's choices become apparent:

- They no longer go to weekly Mass or even on Christmas and Easter.
- They choose not to be married in the Church.

- They don't have their children baptized.
- Their children don't make their first Communion.

They feel as though their children are rejecting the values they worked so hard to instill.

Feelings of betrayal may give way to anger that erupts into loud, angry conversations about the Church and personal experiences.

The best solution is to stop bringing the topic up, to stop pestering or badgering about church.

When anger has subsided, plan a conversation when you and your adult children can share your feelings. Both "sides" need to tell the truth and listen openly, seeking understanding of the other without judgment.

Loving parents and grandparents

want what is best for their children no matter how old the children are. There may be a subtle or not-so-subtle fear for the souls of their offspring. How will they deal with crises in their lives? Even more important, how will they be judged by God?

God is rich in mercy and full of compassion. Be not afraid! God's love and forgiveness is as faithful as that of the prodigal son's father in Luke's Gospel (see 15:11–32). He must have been on the watch for the return of his son.

And even if the son had never returned, the father was no less the parent for keeping watch.

Why Don't They
Go to Church?

Individuation

Maria Montessori is known for her educational methods, particularly with young children. She wrote about the process of *individuation*, in which adolescents become their own persons apart from their parents.

For many, this process is evident when children leave home for college, move to their first apartment, get their first jobs and become self-supporting, or marry.

It's quite natural for adults to wander away from the Church or to search for churches other than the one they grew up with. Setting aside the example of their parents and making their own way—choosing and taking ownership for their own faith life—is an important developmental step.

Many young people take their leave from the Church; some make their way back, and some do not.

They think they don't need it

My first teaching position was in a Catholic high school teaching morality to eleventh-graders. They were wonderful kids from fine families. Day after day they came into my classroom, and day after day their faces were blank.

At the beginning of the second semester, I asked the students what I was doing wrong. One young man raised his hand respectfully and spoke with authority. He stood next to his desk and slowly said, "Miss Latkovich, we just don't need it."

My students had everything they could hope for, so learning about God and the Catholic Church was an academic exercise.

Some years later, I picked up the morning newspaper to read the headline: "Girl on Bicycle Struck and Killed." The driver was that wise young man in my classroom. He wasn't charged, because the little girl had ridden her bike into his path at dusk. When I went to see him, he embraced me warmly and said, "Guess what? Now I need it."

Today, he and his wife and children are active in their parish community.

Issues with Church teaching

What is wrong with the church?

This question is asked many times over, often in courses on ecclesiology—the study of the Church. Lecture halls filled with religious sisters, priests, and laypeople continually analyze this topic.

One professor filled three dry-erase boards with answers offered by the class. Then he asked for a moment of silence.

He returned to the podium and said very slowly and quietly, "What matters most in the Church are simply baptism and Eucharist—and everything else is secondary." What a good lesson.

Nevertheless, arguments continue about the Real Presence in the Eucharist, about birth control, about divorce, about women in ministry, about homosexuality, about forgiveness of sin, and on and on.

For people not practicing the faith, these issues may be the reasons they stay away.

Others feel they lost their Church to Vatican II, which created change in the Church of their childhood. Because the changes of Vatican II were not explained well or encouraged to be studied even by clergy, plenty of leftover wounds keep people away.

All of this can certainly impact one's

"full, conscious, and active" participation in the Mass.

Lack of meaning in the Mass

People who attended Catholic elementary and high school but eventually left the Church are often asked why they don't go to Mass. Many reply, "It's the same show every week."

Even with the changes of the liturgical seasons and the cycles of readings, they can't see enough difference week to week to stay engaged. The weekly celebration of the Eucharist just doesn't stir them. Many begin attending other churches, churches they feel closer to and where they feel interested and engaged.

This is a sad reality. In some Catholic parishes, weekly Mass is not celebrated as it could or should be. The Gospel command to love God and neighbor is sometimes more apparent in other traditions.

Some people stay away because they see a disconnect between the Gospel and the lives of the people who represent the Church or who regularly attend Mass.

When meaning is missing in the celebration of the Eucharist, some turn to the good feelings they get from a worship style that entertains.

The entertainment advantage

Indeed, some worship centers are set up like a theater rather than a holy place. In our technological age, it seems natural to have sound systems and visual effects that can produce spectacular "shows" for worship. This is a great attraction.

Furthermore, in some churches where the emphasis is on the "good life" of the individual churchgoer, the worship service becomes an animated gathering of self-help aficionados.

The messages received at such churches may be very good and helpful, and people are drawn to churches that combine those messages with contemporary music and visuals.

Rejection of the hierarchical, institutional Church

Throughout its history, the Church has had its troubles. Still, our human Church has survived, and sometimes even thrived. Nevertheless, certain issues cause people to reject the hierarchical, institutional Church.

Vatican II clearly states that the Church is the people of God and that the sense of the faithful has a rightful place in Church government. The lack of women and laity in Church governance is very painful for people who feel called to such ministry and service. Feeling minimized and rejected, some of these people find other ways to be nurtured spiritually, other ways to spend their gifts.

We have different thresholds for pain, and sometimes the pain of belonging to a church is more than one can bear. When even good efforts for Church reform are met with rebuke, people feel forced out of the Church.

What You Can and Can't Do to Bring Them Back

Prayer

There is a tradition that Saint Monica prayed that her errant son, Augustine, would come back to the Church. Saint Augustine did indeed return.

The number one suggestion to parents who ask what they can do to bring their children and grandchildren back to the Church is to pray for them.

Timing the invitation

Continue to invite your adult children and grandchildren to join you in worship. The invitation must be sincere and honest, with no "hooks" of guilt. Such invitation and welcome may one day receive a positive response.

But remember, everything happens in God's time. *You* can't make your children start going to Mass, but God can. Certain experiences bring us to God and home to church. The student I spoke of earlier is a good example. He didn't think he needed the Church when he was in high school, but he came home when he experienced a need for God.

Others who experience tragedy may not turn to God but are supported by people of faith who pray on their behalf.

But tragic events aren't the only ones that bring people home. Happy experiences—including marriages, births, and anniversaries—are also the right time to come home to God and Church.

We're better together

Our culture canonizes independence, but community happens from shared story, shared vision, and shared mission. Perhaps our parishes need to be more mindful of each part of building the community of faith, indeed, the body of Christ.

On the night of September 11, 2001, people gathered in churches, synagogues, and mosques all over the United States to mourn and pray *together*. It was a profound event of joining in a time of great need.

Most of the gatherings were in holy places, places where people could feel the presence of God.

Many parishioners come to life when they make the connection between shared story, shared vision, and shared mission. For example, out of the Gospel stories of loving God and neighbor, youth groups become mission-focused. A community of young people comes together to serve.

Such community is where good worship experience begins.

Celebrating sacraments

The sacraments are the way we in the Roman Catholic Church worship. Each sacrament represents a significant moment of life.

The best we can do to evangelize or welcome back those who have been away is to celebrate the sacraments with heart—with meaning—as a community of faith.

Too many times people say, "I don't get anything out of it." And too often they are right.

The word *liturgy* means the "work of the people." So it's not simply up to the pastor. Emphasizing good liturgy—music, lectors, homily, environment—will bring people back, just as a business that builds a good reputation maintains and grows its customer base. With good liturgy, the community of faith is built and is happy to come together to celebrate.

Relationships with pastoral folks

We are formed by the company we keep. One of my students worked at the local city hall. After about six weeks, one of her sisters mentioned that her language had gotten foul. My student was startled but recognized that she had unknowingly picked up the habits of the people she worked with each day. It took a conscious effort on her part to use only language she was proud of.

But it works both ways: We also pick up *good* habits from one another. Your children can observe you, your relationships in the community of faith, and the great benefits you receive from believing in God and worshiping in a parish community.

Don't Lose Heart

When the people of ancient Israel were overwhelmed with the demands of the law, the prophet Micah wrote, "You have been told, O man, what is good, and what the LORD requires of you: Only to do the right and to love goodness, and to walk humbly with your God" (6:8).

The Gospel of Matthew teaches that when Jesus was asked to name the greatest commandment, he proclaimed, "You shall love the Lord, your God, with all your heart, with all your soul, and with all your mind. This is the greatest and the first commandment. The second is like it: You shall love your neighbor as yourself" (22:37–39).

Neither of these teachings says anything about going to church. Those of us baptized into Christ who are faithful members of the Church community find meaning in our membership through the celebration of sacraments, the liturgy of the Eucharist, social events, group outings, Bible-study groups, watching and playing sports, service projects, and so on.

May all of our children and grand-children abide by the commandments articulated by both Micah and Jesus. May we always keep them in our hearts and prayers and entrust them to our good and gracious God.

Prayer for
Your Children

O Creator God,
I praise and bless you
for the gift of my children.
Give me the grace to love them
as you do:

With patience,
when my impatience rises,
With kindness,
when I might withhold care,
With understanding,
when I am tempted to judge,
With acceptance,
when I would reject.

Give me words that are ever
affirming of my children,
even if I cannot affirm their
choices or actions.

Show me how to forgive
in word and in deed
and to always provide a home
and heart where they are
welcome and feel safe.

In all difficulties,
help me remember that
my children are your own.
I do want to place them
in your hands and care,
for there are times
when I can do no more.

Abide with them and with me
as I pray in the name of Jesus
and his parents on earth,
Mary and Joseph.
Amen.